Twenty-Five Years On

Twenty-Five Years On

A Message for Today

1979-2004

With a Foreword by
Archbishop Seán Brady

VERITAS

Published 2004 by
Veritas Publications
7/8 Lower Abbey Street
Dublin 1
Email publications veritas.ie
Website www.veritas.ie
In association with the Catholic Communications Office

ISBN 1 85390 806 1

10 9 8 7 6 5 4 3 2 1

A catalogue record for this book is available from the British Library.

Designed by Colette Dower
Printed in the Republic of Ireland by Betaprint Ltd, Dublin

Veritas books are printed on paper made from the wood pulp of managed forests. For every tree felled, at least one tree is planted, thereby renewing natural resources.

Contents

Pope John Paul II visited Ireland
from 29 September to 1 October 1979.
The quotes included in this book
are taken from various addresses and homilies
given by his Holiness in Dublin, Drogheda,
Clonmacnois, Galway, Knock, Limerick,
Maynooth and Shannon.

Foreword

There are some questions, which, I imagine, sooner or later, all who think for themselves will ask. Where do I come from? Why do I exist? What are my relationships with the invisible world? How must I behave in order to achieve the goal of my life? Why am I subject to suffering and death? What hope have I in the face of these realities? I cannot think of any questions which are more relevant to life.

The Church brings God's answers to these questions. It spreads the Good News that there are answers to these essential questions, and that God has answered all of these questions with a gift of truth and life that surpasses our deepest expectations.

Over the past twenty-five years Pope John Paul II has repeated and explained and clarified these answers. In doing so he speaks not only with the authority of his office as the Bishop of Rome and Successor of Peter, but with the human authority and authenticity of a highly intelligent man who has absorbed and internalised God's message through prayer and study. The Pope can communicate that message because he knows the human heart, he understands contemporary culture and has an intimate personal relationship with Jesus Christ.

It was a great grace that Pope John Paul decided to visit Ireland so early in his pontificate. During his three-day visit in 1979 he delivered several talks, sermons and addresses. In doing so he was fulfilling his role as Chief Teacher in the Church and seeking to deepen its life through a better knowledge of our Risen Lord and Saviour.

I welcome the decision of Veritas to publish *Twenty-Five Years On – A Message for Today*, a selection of quotations taken from the various addresses and homilies given by the Pope in Dublin, Drogheda, Clonmacnois, Galway, Knock, Maynooth, Limerick and Shannon. The words and the photographs will evoke powerful memories of those glorious days.

The intervening twenty-five years have been a time of immense change throughout the world. In a time of fast and furious change we all need sure points of reference. Pope John Paul came to Ireland on a pastoral visit. His goal was to promote our full well-being by providing solid and secure points of reference and to assist us in the ongoing conversion that is a central part of Christian life. This he did mainly through his preaching and teaching. His message continues to be relevant today because it is the message of Jesus Christ – who is the same yesterday, today and forever.

'Christ has the answer to your questions and the key to history; he has the power to uplift hearts.'
(p.17)

This book in many respects summarises and encapsulates the central themes of the reign of a Pope who will surely be judged by scholars and commentators to have made a defining contribution to the Church and to the world at a critical time in history, spanning two centuries and two millennia. This book will be enjoyed by anyone who seeks to relive those special days in 1979 or who seeks to inform themselves of the teachings of Pope John Paul II. It will be a very useful aid for teachers and preachers. I hope that many people will read it and use it.

+ Seán Brady

Archbishop of Armagh
President, Irish Bishops' Conference

The Call to Faith

Faith and fidelity are marks of the Church in Ireland, a Church of martyrs, a Church of witnesses; a Church of heroic faith, heroic fidelity. These are the historical signs marking the track of faith on Irish soil. The Gospel and the Church have struck deep roots in the soul of the Irish people.

The word of God is worthy of all our efforts. To embrace it in its purity and integrity, and to spread it by word and example is a great mission. And this is your mission, today and tomorrow and for the rest of your lives. Something else is needed: something that you will find only in Christ, for he alone is the measure and the scale that you must use to evaluate your own life. In Christ, you will discover the true greatness of your own humanity; he will make you understand your own dignity as human beings 'created to the image and likeness of God' (Gen 1:26). Christ has the answers to your questions and the key to history; he has the power to uplift hearts.

What I really want you to realise is this: that God counts on you: that he makes his plans, in a way, dependent on your free collaboration, on the oblation of your lives, and on the generosity with which you follow the inspirations of the Holy Spirit in the depths of your hearts.

Our desire for Christian unity springs from a need to be faithful to the will of God, as revealed in Christ. Our unity in Christ, moreover, conditions the effectiveness of our evangelisation; it determines the credibility of our witness before the world. Christ prayed for the unity of his disciples, precisely 'so that the world may believe'.

(John 17)

Despite our human weakness and our sins, despite all obstacles, we accept in humility and faith the great principle enunciated by our Saviour: 'What is impossible with men is possible with God'.

(Luke 18:27)

Benvenuto in Irlanda Al Papa

Whenever we have questions, whenever we are burdened, whenever we are faced with the choices that our faith imposes on us, the word of the Lord will comfort and guide us.

When we look at the works of faith, we must give thanks to God. Thanks to God for the saints and apostles and all who were the instruments for implanting and keeping alive this faith, and who have 'done God's will throughout the ages'. Thanks to God for the generosity of faith that brought forth fruits of justice and holiness to life. Thanks to God for the preservation of the faith in integrity and purity of teaching. Thanks to God for the continuity of the message of the apostles handed down intact to this day.

The basis of our personal identity, of our common bond and of our ministry is found in Jesus Christ, the Son of God and High Priest of the New Testament. For this reason, brethren, my first exhortation as I come among you today is this:
'Let us keep our eyes fixed on Jesus, who inspires and perfects our faith' (Heb 12:2).
Since we are pastors of this flock, we must indeed look to him who is the chief Shepherd to enlighten us, to sustain us, and to give us joy as we serve the flock, leading it 'in paths of righteousness for his name's sake' (Ps 23:3).

What a great grace it is for the entire Christian world that, in this our day, the Holy Spirit has powerfully stirred up in human hearts a real desire for this 'newness of life'. And what a great gift of God it is that there exists today among Christians a deeper realisation of the need to be perfectly one in Christ and in his Church: to be one, in accordance with Christ's own prayer, even as he and his Father are one.

(John: 17)

All Christians, incorporated into Christ and his Church by baptism, are consecrated to God. They are called to profess the faith which they have received. By the sacrament of confirmation, they are further endowed by the Holy Spirit with special strength to be witnesses of Christ and sharers in his mission of salvation. Every lay Christian is therefore an extraordinary work of God's grace and is called to the heights of holiness. Sometimes, lay men and women do not seem to appreciate to the full the dignity and the vocation that is theirs as lay people. No, there is no such thing as an 'ordinary layman', for all of you have been called to conversion through the death and resurrection of Jesus Christ. As God's holy people you are called to fulfill your role in the evangelisation of the world.

Dear brothers and sisters, every act of reverence, every genuflexion that you make before the Blessed Sacrament, is important because it is an act of faith in Christ, an act of love for Christ. And every sign of the cross and gesture of respect made each time you pass a church is also an act of faith.

Parenthood

Dear fathers and mothers of Ireland, believe in your vocation, that beautiful vocation of marriage and parenthood which God has given to you. Believe that God is with you – for all parenthood in heaven and on earth takes its name from him. Do not think that anything you will do in life is more important than to be a good Christian father and mother.

Peace and Justice

corpus sumite sanctum bibentes quo
et sanguine a quo refecti
dominus ipse sacerdos

Faith and social ethics demand from us respect for the established State authorities. But this respect also finds its expression in individual acts of mediation, in persuasion, in moral influence, and indeed in firm requests. For while it is true, as St Paul says, that he who is in authority bears the sword (Rom 13:4), which we renounce in accordance with the clear recommendation of Christ to Peter in the Garden of Gethsemane (Mt 26:52), nevertheless, precisely because we are defenceless, we have a special right and duty to influence those who wield the sword of authority. There are deeper reasons and stronger laws to which men, nations and peoples are subject. It is for us to discern these reasons and in their light to become, before those in authority, spokesmen for the moral order. This order is superior to force and violence. In this superiority of the moral order is expressed all the dignity of men and nations.

The witness to faith in Christ which we share with our brethren must continue to find expression not only in prayer for full unity but also in prayer and sustained effort for reconciliation and peace in this beloved land. The union of endeavour must lead us to take into consideration the whole mechanism of strife, cruelty, and growing hatred, in order to 'overcome evil with good'.

(Rom 12:12)

The moral law, guardian of human rights, protector of the dignity of man, cannot be set aside by any person or group, or by the State itself, for any cause, not even for security or in the interests of law and order. The law of God stands in judgement over all reasons of State. As long as injustices exist in any of the areas that touch upon the dignity of the human person, be it in the political, social or economic field, be it in the cultural or religious sphere, true peace will not exist. Peace cannot be established by violence, peace can never flourish in a climate of terror, intimidation and death. It is Jesus himself who said: 'All who take the sword will perish by the sword' (Mt 25:52).

I proclaim, with the conviction of my faith in Christ and with an awareness of my mission, that violence is evil, that violence is unacceptable as a solution to problems, that violence is unworthy of man. Violence is a lie, for it goes against the truth of our faith, the truth of our humanity. Violence destroys what it claims to defend: the dignity, the life, the freedom of human beings. Violence is a crime against humanity, for it destroys the very fabric of society. I pray with you that the moral sense and Christian conviction of Irish men and women may never become obscured and blunted by the lie of violence, that nobody may ever call murder by any other name than murder, that the spiral of violence may never be given the distinction of unavoidable logic of necessary retaliation.

Never before in the history of mankind has peace been so much talked about and so ardently desired as in our day. The growing interdependence of peoples and nations makes almost everyone subscribe – at least in principle – to the ideal of universal human brotherhood. Great international institutions debate humanity's peaceful coexistence. Public opinion is growing in consciousness of the absurdity of war as a means to resolve differences. More and more, peace is seen as a necessary condition to fraternal relations among nations, and among peoples. Peace is more and more clearly seen as the only way to justice; peace is itself the work of justice.

Christianity does not command us to close our eyes to difficult human problems. It does not permit us to neglect and refuse to see unjust social or international situations. What Christianity does forbid is to seek solutions to these situations by ways of hatred, by murdering of defenceless people, by methods of terrorism. Let me say more: Christianity understands and recognises the noble and just struggle for justice; but Christianity is decisively opposed to fomenting hatred and to provoking violence or struggle for the sake of 'struggle'. The command, 'thou shalt not kill', must be binding on the conscience of humanity, if the terrible destiny of Cain is not to be repeated.

You heard the words of Jesus: 'Love your enemies.' The command of Jesus does not mean that we are not bound by love for our native land; it does not mean that we can remain indifferent before injustice in its various temporal and historical aspects. These words of Jesus take away only hate. I beg you to reflect deeply: what would human life be if Jesus had not spoken such words? What would the world be if in our mutual relations we were to give primacy to hatred among people, between classes, between nations? What would the future of humanity be if we were to base on this hatred the future of individuals and nations?

You cannot be a genuine Christian on Sunday, unless you try to be true to Christ's spirit also in your work, your commercial dealings, at your trade union or your employers' or professional meetings. How can you be a true community in Christ at Mass unless you try to think of the welfare of the whole national community when decisions are being taken by your particular sector or group? How can you be ready to meet Christ in judgement unless you remember how the poor are affected by the behaviour of your group or by your personal life style? For the Christ will say to us all: 'In so far as you did this to one of the least of these brothers of mine, you did it to me'.

(Mt 25:40)

Many people now are tempted to self-indulgence and consumerism, and ones identity is often defined by what one owns. Prosperity and affluence, even when they are only beginning to be available to larger strata of society, tend to make people assume that they have a right to all that prosperity can bring, and thus they can become selfish in their demands... The challenge that is already with us is the temptation to accept as true freedom what in reality is only a new form of slavery. Reaching the goals of justice in the economic and social fields will require that religious convictions and fervour be not separated from a moral and social conscience.

A United Christian Church

Let no one ever doubt the commitment of the Catholic Church and of the Apostolic See of Rome to the pursuit of the unity of the Church of Christians. The movement towards unity must not stop until it has reached its goal. The Catholic Church, faithful to the direction taken at the Council, not only wants to go forward on the way that leads to the restoration of unity, but is anxious, according to its means and in full submission to the promptings of the Holy Spirit, to strengthen on every level its contribution to this great movement of all Christians.

Our desire for Christian unity springs from a need to be faithful to the will of God, as revealed in Christ. Our unity in Christ, moreover, conditions the effectiveness of our evangelisation; it determines the credibility of our witness before the world. Christ prayed for the unity of his disciples, precisely 'so that the world may believe'.

(John 17)

The Gospel reading tells us of Jesus as 'the Good Shepherd', whose one desire is to bring all together in one flock. I come to you in his name, in the name of Jesus Christ, who died in order 'to come into one the children of God who scattered abroad'.

(John 11:52)

Saint Peter says that Christians are a 'royal priesthood, a holy nation' (1 Pet 2:9). All Christians, incorporated into Christ and his Church by baptism, are consecrated to God. They are called to profess the faith which they have received. By the sacrament of confirmation, they are further endowed by the Holy Spirit.

What a great grace it is for the entire Christian world that, in this our day, the Holy Spirit has powerfully stirred up in human hearts a real desire for this 'newness of life'. And what a great gift of God it is that there exists today among Christians a deeper realisation of the need to be perfectly one in Christ and in his Church: to be one in accordance with Christ's own prayer, even as he and his Father are one.

(John 17)

Suffering and Pain

Although I cannot take away your suffering and your pain, I can assure you, in the name of the Lord, how important a contribution you can make to the Church, to the kingdom of God. When your patience and pain are united with the suffering of Christ, when they are accepted out of love, then they take on a value they never had before. They help in bringing salvation and holiness to the world. Suffering is difficult. Only love can make it easy, and perfect love can make it joy.

By his suffering and death Jesus took on himself all human suffering, and he gave it a new value. As a matter of fact, he calls upon the sick, upon everyone who suffers, to collaborate with him in the salvation of the world. Your call to suffering requires strong faith and patience. Yes, it means that you are called to love with a special intensity. But remember that our Blessed Mother, Mary, is close to you, just as she was close to Jesus at the foot of the cross. And she will never leave you all alone.

Youth

I believe in youth. I believe in youth with all my heart and with all the strength of my conviction. And today I say; I believe in the youth of Ireland! Like other young people of your age in other countries, you are affected by what is happening in society around you. Although you still live in an atmosphere where true religious and moral principles are held in honour, you have to realise that your fidelity to these principles will be tested in many ways. A society that has lost its higher religious and moral principles will become an easy prey for manipulation and for domination by the forces, which, under the pretext of greater freedom, will enslave even more.

Prayer

May our ears constantly hear the proper clarity of your motherly voice: 'Do whatever my Son tells you.' Enable us to persevere with Christ. Enable us, Mother of the Church, to build up his Mystical Body by living with the life that he alone can grant us from his fullness, which is both divine and human.

Christ, Prince of Peace; Mary, Mother of Peace, Queen of Ireland; St Patrick, St Oliver, and all saints of Ireland; I together with all those gathered here and with all who join with me, invoke you, Watch over Ireland. Protect humanity. Amen.

F5

We entrust and consecrate to you, Mother of Christ and Mother of the Church, our hearts, our consciences, and our works, in order that they may be in keeping with the faith we profess. We entrust and consecrate to you each and every one of those who make up both the community of the Irish people and the community of the people of God living in this land.

Priesthood

To be with the Lord is always also to be sent by him to do his work. A priest is called by Christ; a priest is with Christ; a priest is sent by Christ. A priest is sent in the power of the same Holy Spirit which drove Jesus untiringly along the roads of life, the roads of history. Whatever the difficulties, the disappointments, the set-backs, we priests find in Christ and in the power of his Spirit the strength to 'struggle wearily on helped only by his power driving us irresistibly'.

(Col 1:2)

Marriage

Míle Fáilte
GALWAY
1979
BELFAST

Married people must believe in the power of the sacrament to make them holy; they must believe in their vocation to witness through marriage the power of Christ's love. True love and the grace of God can never let marriage become a self-centred relationship of two individuals, living side by side for their own interests.

The Eucharist

Whether we serve in politics, in the economic, cultural, social or scientific fields – no matter what our occupation is – the Eucharist is a challenge to our daily lives. Dear brothers and sisters! There must always be consistency between what we believe and what we do. We cannot live on the glories of our past Christian history. Our union with Christ in the Eucharist must be expressed in the truth of our lives today – in our actions, in our behaviour, in our lifestyle, and in our relationship with others. For each one of us the Eucharist is a call to ever greater effort, so that we may live as true followers of Jesus: truthful in our speech, generous in our deeds, concerned, respectful of the dignity and rights of all persons, whatever their rank or income, self-sacrificing, fair and just, kind, considerate, compassionate and self-controlled – looking to the well-being of our families, our young people, our country, Europe and the world.

OLY CROSS
RDOYNE

From the upper room in Jerusalem, from the last supper, in a certain sense, the Eucharist writes the history of human hearts and of human communities. Let us reflect on all those, who, being nourished on the body and blood of the Lord, have lived and died on this island, bearing in themselves, because of the Eucharist, the pledge of eternal life. Let us think of so many generations of sons and daughters of this country, and at the same time, sons and daughters of the Church.

The sacrifice of the body and blood of Jesus Christ offered up for us is an act of supreme love on the part of the Saviour. It is his great victory over sin and death – a victory that he communicates to us. The Eucharist is a promise of eternal life, since Jesus himself tells us: 'He who eats my flesh and drinks my blood has eternal life, and I will raise him up at the last day' (John 6:54). The holy sacrifice of the Mass is meant to be the festive celebration of our salvation. In the Mass we give thanks and praise to God our Father for having given us the redemption through the precious blood of Jesus Christ. The Eucharist is also the centre of the Church's unity, as well as her greatest treasure. In the words of the Second Vatican Council, the Eurcharist contains 'the Church's entire spiritual wealth' (*Presbyterorum Ordinis*, 5).

ST. MATTHEW'S
KILMARNOCK
KNOCK 1979
SCOTLAND

The Eucharist is also a great call to conversion. We know that it is an invitation to the banquet; that, by nourishing ourselves on the Eucharist, we receive in it the body and blood of Christ, under the appearances of bread and wine. Precisely because of this invitation, the Eucharist is and remains the call to conversion. If we receive it as such a call, such an invitation, it brings forth in us its proper fruits. It transforms our lives.

Forgiveness

Because of Christ's love and mercy, there is no sin that is too great to be forgiven; there is no sinner who will be rejected. Every person who repents will be received by Jesus Christ with forgiveness and love.

Even when our belief in the fundamental goodness of every human being has been shaken or undermined, even if long-held convictions and attitudes have hardened our hearts, there is one source of power that is stronger than every disappointment, bitterness or ingrained mistrust, and that power is Jesus Christ, who brought forgiveness and reconciliation to the world. Teach your children how to forgive, make your homes places of love and forgiveness; make your streets and neighbourhoods centres of peace and reconciliation.

Every time we receive the sacrament of penance or reconciliation, we receive the forgiveness of Christ, and we know that this forgiveness comes to us through the merits of his death – the very death that we celebrate in the Eucharist. In the sacrament of reconciliation, we are invited to meet Christ personally in this way, and to do so frequently.

Love

Communities who stand together in their acceptance of Jesus' supreme message of love, expressed in peace and reconciliation, and in their rejection of all violence, constitute an irresistible force for achieving what many have come to accept as impossible.

Sometimes, one could have the feeling that, before the experiences of history and before concrete situations, love has lost its power and that it is impossible to practise it. And yet, in the long run, love always brings victory, love is never defeated.

St Patrick

St Patrick was not only the first Primate of Ireland, but he also was the one who succeeded in implanting a religious tradition in the Irish soul, in such a way that all Irish Christians can rightly glory in the heritage of St Patrick. He was truly Irish, he was truly Christian; and the Irish people have preserved this same heritage of his through many centuries of challenges, suffering, and social and political upheavals, thereby setting an example for all who believe that the message of Christ enhances and strengthens the most profound aspirations of people for dignity, fraternal unity and truth.

Acknowledgements

Photography from the following sources:

Robert Allen Photography:
pages 18, 20, 34, 42, 46 and 68; used with permission.

The Archdiocese of Armagh:
front cover, pages 2-3, 10, 16, 22, 24, 26, 28, 56, 58, 62, 64, 66, 70, pages 74-122 and pages 127-127; used with permission.

The private collection of Bishop John Magee:
pages 30, 32, 38, 44, 46, 48, 50, 52 and 54; used with permission.

Patrick Lavelle, Knock Shrine Bureau, Knock:
page 14; used with permission.

Eoin Fegan: back cover; used with permission.

Veritas would like also like to thank Irene Stevenson from *The Irish Times* and the staff at the *The Irish Catholic* for their help.

Photos of Pope John Paul II

Maynooth
front cover, pages 2-3

Dublin
back cover, pages 10, 16, 18, 20, 22, 24, 26, 28, 30, 34, 38, 42, 44, 46, 48, 50, 52, 56, 58, 62, 64, 66, 68 and 70

Knock
pages 14, 106, 110, 112, 114 and 122

Drogheda
pages 74, 76, 80 and 96

Clonmacnois
pages 30 & 32

Limerick
pages 84, 86, 102 and 104

Galway
pages 54, 88, 92, 96, 100, 118 and 126-127